Ghost Warrior

Ghost Warrior

by

Robert Sasse

COMBAT MARINE
VIETNAM 1966-67

Red Nest Publishing
PO Box 43
Gila NM 88038

RobertSasse4@hotmail.com

DEDICATION

To warriors from all wars,
may we all find peace.

CONTENTS

CONTENTS

INTRODUCTION

The Power to Take Life, The Power to Give Life

Both before and for many years after, I could not have guessed that my time as a combat Marine in Vietnam would define my future and ultimately lead to a life view I might otherwise have missed. Those few months of my youth were filled with terror and exhilaration. Many years later the phrase, "when boys with guns were gods" seemed to define the false sense of power and immortality that we carried in the face of violent death and bodily mayhem.

I returned from Vietnam and soon discovered that it was not possible to rewrap myself in the swaddling of a Montana childhood. Combat experiences had interposed between who I had been as a rancher's son and the angry young man that came home from war. Everything was the same, but different. All of life was seen through a thousand yard stare and what I saw had irreparably changed.

I was restless and jumpy and could not get comfortable in the place where I had been raised by loving parents and caring neighbors. I started drinking to

1

squelch a pain I didn't understand and after a big fight in the local bar, I packed up and moved twenty-five hundred miles to Fairbanks, Alaska hoping that geography would still the roiling in my gut. It didn't. In that beautiful, wild and remote place that Alaska is, my mind was churning full time trying to resolve the deaths and mayhem I had been a part of. I tried to rinse the bitterness from my life with too much booze, only compounding my confusion.

As years passed my ability to function deteriorated. A first marriage began and ended. With another try at changing geography, I moved to Alberta, Canada. A second marriage produced four kids and a relationship constantly stretched to breaking by my thoughts of suicide, skirmishes with the law and an inability to provide for my family. A last attempt at running from problems took me to Omaha, Nebraska. A simmering rage had become the ruling emotion of my life and I was so volatile that hiding in my basement and crawling around in the bushes at night along the Missouri River seemed the only safe things to do.

With much help, I was able to break the shackles of alcoholism and eventually led to professional help in the VA hospital system to deal with the residue of Vietnam experiences. That meant facing and looking at painful memories I had worked hard to ignore.

Though I dealt with many more, three incidents seem to illustrate the core of my confliction. We were near the demilitarized zone between North and South Vietnam. The area was full of North Vietnamese Army regulars, well equipped and excellently trained. We were moving rapidly through a fortified area to help another unit. Rounding a bend in the trail, I saw a hand protruding from a shallow and hastily dug grave. As I got closer, half the face of a Vietnamese boy, who might have been as young as fifteen, showed through the jungle dirt. Little bits of rotted leaves and black soil stuck to his smooth skin and the contrast emphasized his youth. Someone had closed his eyes and I remember thinking that a friend must have risked his own life taking the time to dig that shallow grave.

Later, during an ambush that hit my company, a friend and I crawled down a hill to retrieve a wounded Marine. Washutt was from Sheridan, Wyoming and the proximity to my home in Montana had tied us as buddies in the few months we were together. As Washutt crawled in the dark behind me, his hand brushed my leg as a burst of machine gun fire raked the hill around us. Washutt was dead, killed by that machine gun burst. In the dark of many nights since, I have felt the touch of his hand on my leg.

Toward the end of my tour, I made a trip from our combat perimeter to the relative civility of the airstrip at Da Nang. That was a land of milk and honey for those of us who lived and fought in jungles and rice paddies. Ice cream, cold sodas and hot chow from a real mess hall were all available. I wandered, gaping at the goodies until I rounded the corner of a building and saw a row of Vietnamese prisoners sitting on the hot tarmac, blindfolded and trussed. They were guarded and watched over by two humorless military policemen who were quick to prod and threaten. Some sat defiantly stoic and unmoving; others trembled in the heat of that boiling afternoon. My vivid recollection is seeing a puddle of urine spreading between the legs of an old woman and feeling for a moment the humiliation and terror she must have felt. That scene provided a stark understanding of the ugliness of war.

Those three incidents contrasted with my youth where I was raised on a ranch cradled in the foothills and valleys of the Crazy Mountains of Montana. I grew up in the rhythm of life and death on that ranch where cattle and game animals were killed for meat, sick and wounded creatures were destroyed to prevent suffering and the spread of disease. Animals regarded as varmints were dispatched on sight.

When I was ten, my dog Poncho had two legs cut off by a hay mower. My father and I followed him under the porch where he had managed to crawl. I held a flashlight while Dad shot him. As I grew older, twelve or thirteen, it became my job to do the killing. I learned to take life without conscious thoughts of morality. I was surprised by a neighbor, who after climbing onto the corral fence and shooting a steer he had raised said, "That's like shooting an old friend." I did not yet understand the compassion that went with the responsibilities of life and death.

It was that attitude I carried into the Marine Corps. There we were trained in the art of taking life and encouraged to relish the thought of destroying our enemies. By the time the big orange and white Braniff Airliner hit the tarmac in DaNang, South Vietnam, I was ready to rush off the plane, bayoneted rifle in hand and begin dispatching all who stood as enemies of my country. Fortunately, it didn't work that way. I had no rifle and they weren't waiting.

It wasn't long before I was hugging the mud in rice paddies and shooting at unseen bad guys in tree lines and jungle. I approached combat with the dictates of my training; kill, kill, kill, convinced I was saving people at home from the horrors of communism.

I came home understanding that a line had been crossed. On one side was the innocence of taking human life, on the other, the innocence was gone and to my horror, I discovered the line no longer existed. The choice to kill or not now required the conscious thought that only in combat did the rules allow taking of life. What an awesome awareness.

Later, after sobriety and much therapy, those vivid images of the enemy soldier, my friend, and the prisoners, worked their way into my psyche and awakened new feelings regarding life.

Albert Whitehat Sr., a respected elder and teacher of the Lakota Sioux language, says all things have the power to take life and give life. Consider a stone or water, both of which obviously contain the power of life and death in many ways. A tree, the wind, the sun, all imbued with that power. We, as humans share that awesome power. Harmony in our lives is finding a balance of those powers as we walk our path.

Today I try to be a giver of life. I live with my wonderful wife in New Mexico where we try to help others find harmony in their lives. I live in peace, not as a conscientious objector to war but rather as someone who has found a balance between taking life and giving life. It was, in the end, the out of balance experience of war that gave me this invaluable lesson and for that I am now grateful.

Robert Sasse

GHOST WARRIOR

From ugly fields of war,
from death and pain
and churning gut,
from places humanity

no longer finds,
from screaming child
and dying foe, from reflections
of grime coated soul,

the warrior walks
to find his home and heart
and leaves behind
a wandering ghost

who holds him from his task.

THE MULTIPLEGIC

Thumbnail against gut-gray back,
a centipede screams and drags thirty-two
useless legs across the lip of my foxhole.

Rising from ashes of scorched earth,
I climb through the naked bamboo
of defoliated jungle to speak
unspeakables about bastard war.
Swaddling's of my guilt fall away at the feet
of those who still believe in politick.

I whistle a private national anthem
whose chorus is about freedom of my soul.
I borrow words from poets and think
in the language of jungle fighters,
a voice of passion.
Not noise of love makers on clean sheets,
but quiet passion of old ladies carrying rice
to babies who cry in dusty corners.

In a marble pagoda near the southeast corner
of my soul, names are whispered of killed,
wounded, missing, forgotten,
lonely and hopeless heroes.
On a blank wall, unnamed children of long
dead warriors remain, silently unnamed.

Lament is wasted on those who don't hear.
not hearing, they don't care who sobs loudest.
I speak to the undrafted, untrained killers
who will practice folly in another field.
I cry for the centipede.

A POEM ABOUT A POEM
ABOUT YOUR WALL

A girl paid tribute to your wall
    with chiseled words and shameless tears.
    She said neither the war nor the wall were hers
    until she bravely owned them both
    when your names touched her eyes.

She spoke gently of flowing forms --
    granite rising from damp earth
    and returning like you and
    her emotion roiled up and flowed across
    the graveyards where you rest.

All the angry shards of cutting metal
    that once tore through your ripened flesh
    could not etch the real wall of Life and Death
    like the slow tears from her knowing eyes,
    her heart a pounding chisel as she spoke.

The world will walk by your wall as she did--
    in silent pain and reverent awe
    and for that little time they will
    watch you rise again as your quiet
    names speak loudly of senseless war.

REAL WAR

Bob K. walked from teenage streets
into warrior jungles.
He taunted life in both places.
One day a silver capsule,
devil spawn of a US Navy plane,
fell end over end to explode
like a bitch's tongue at his feet.
Gelled gasoline steals oxygen.
Lungs collapse. Eyes bulge
in horrid white stares.
Dehydrated tissue
and crispy patches of skin
become gaping mummies.

Linda R. asked if her Bobby suffered much.

DEATH OF DEER HUNTING

4:00 AM, four pieces of bacon from the
smokehouse, three large tan eggs, one white
pullet egg gathered last night from the chicken
coop, two slices of Mom's fresh bread,
homemade butter, gooseberry jelly
(remembering tart berries from a pail),
all eaten with an eighteen-year-old
early morning appetite.

An inch of fresh snow, means good tracking.
The Power Wagon's six-volt eyes
see a wire gate on a cow trail road.
At the Walker homestead, an owl flies from the
falling barn, across sweet, new snow.
We park in the grove of quakin' asp'
by the wooden fence.

We wear heavy Pac's and wool sox with
red-banded tops pulled over Levi legs,
blanket lined Carhartt jackets,
monkey faced gloves, a red cap with flaps that
subscribe to game laws.
Snow underfoot, our steps sound like
eating crisp celery.
Damp sagebrush scrapes our legs
in the darkness as we climb uphill,
along the south bank of the creek.

In grey predawn mountain light
a two-point buck starts close by as he
finds our smell.
Our steps freeze as we stare at the ghost deer.
Farther up the ridge, a mossy horn steps out.
I count seven points through the Bosch and
Lomb 4X scope.

Careful, step by slow step, we go down wind,
over the granite slide rock.
Straight above, a magnificent rack,
swollen neck. I chamber a .270 cartridge
and bring the barrel down, cross hairs
behind the skull, I squeeze the trigger gently.

Neck shots cause a slow gagging rattle,
head shots--drop like stones,
gut shots burn, the wounded scream,
blood filled holes are gaped at in disbelief.
Jungle fighters don't aim discriminately,
I had to tell Carroll his leg was gone.

Robert Sasse

SHARING AN UGLY SECRET FROM VIETNAM WITH A FRIEND

On a fall Topeka sidewalk
two transient leaves twist and roll
along a gaping gutter,
washing past brown and brittle swans
floating on Gage Park Pond.
Dusty gusts slap at cold stone walls
as frayed and yellow edges
bend rapidly across drying lawns
to find concrete corners on the capitol steps.

At the stoplight
I whispered to Joe, "when I pulled
the trigger his chest fell hard beneath
my foot and he made an awful sound,
like when Dad ran over my dog with the
tractor."

PTSD

Walls stare and
circled eyes
stare back
a thousand yards
through
thick molasses days
and broken nights

Storms rage
and taunt
'til withered anger
dies on broken stones
bleeding
without
sound

New days
fall on shards
of yesterdays
shattered masks
and shattered walls
that only worked
a little while

Staring back
into days before
and days after
seeing only
circled eyes.

Robert Sasse

RIVER ICE IN EARLY WINTER

Armadas of ice ships slide by,
silent against cold Missouri gray.
Omaha sleeps in frosty moonlight
behind winter bones of frozen trees.
I am tempted to commandeer an ice flow
and join this frozen navy, steaming south.

A circle of ice collides with the riverbank
beneath my feet. Turning slowly,
attempting to regain the channel,
more ice rams it back into the trap.
A prisoner locked in helpless swirls –
each chance to escape ruined
by endless islands rushing by.

I want to cheat,
to push the ice with my stick,
but I stand silently
watching a drama not mine.

ON A MONSOON NIGHT

I saw you today humpin' down the road,
tired eyes focused on battlefields somewhere else.
We passed before on a monsoon night
or a microwaved day and stared thousand yard
stares at each other.

Your soul smells like jungle ooze
and mine is full of mud
and hung with slimy leeches.
Remember once when we carried our innocence
in jungle slings?
I knew you when you held your buddy while he
died his warrior's death.

I wasn't there, I had my own dying to watch
but we both heard his screams in the fifth round
of a twelve round nightmare.
I heard you whistling up route nine
and down the dim lit path to America's
consciousness.

And now through state of the art dead reckoning
(or reckoning with the dead) we're here.
We *lurped stateside with ringed eyes, hot startle
responses and camouflaged feelings.

$\rightarrow$

Robert Sasse

Just another battle. We broke through perimeters
guarding against baby killers and drug crazed
social rejects.

Shit man! It wasn't our first hot landing or
our first ambush. Now the wire's up around our
souls and we're still digging in or digging out.
We were there brother. Welcome home!

**lurp - *long range recon patrol*

MY FATHER'S LAND

I taste the soil with feet bared
and walk in shadows of pine trees
stretching from hilltops to sweet blue sky.
These mountains stood watch
while I was born.

My father worked the soil
and returned to dust, though before he died he
laid seed beneath his feet
in a sacred way. He caressed the land
as he lived beneath its trees.
It was enough for him to wake each day
beneath Montana's bright and open sky.

He left me promise under that shielding sky
though I left to make my mark in other dust
and battle my own beliefs with
the help of small men in sandaled feet.
I lost myself under foreign trees
so thick and tangled there was no land.

So I cried for my father's land and
I longed for his ways as I wandered beneath
a sky churned white with death,
my soul defoliated like the trees.
My life became the dirt
that churned beneath my feet.
I came to hate the day that I was born.

$\rightarrow$

Yet in some broken night was born a yearning
to return to that childhood land
and shake the past,
to clean from my feet all foreign clay
and rest where my father lay
in dust beneath his trees.

I suppose the story might end in those trees
when I found life again except I couldn't stay.
I took wing and didn't land once
but landed here and there
under many skies that slowed my mind,
but not my feet.

Now I stand where my father's feet
once walked behind his plow.
Not on that soil, but I know
soil tended by him will forever
cling to my wandering shoes.

CATHARSIS

His chair tipped against the wall as he stared empty-eyed into the dusty leaves of a plastic palm tree leaning on the corner of the stage.

He was a freak that stood out in a room full of freaks. A faded and torn military field jacket hung from his skinny, meatless shoulders. A pair of greasy, lifeless Wrangler jeans was stuffed into unlaced jungle boots that looked as though they might have just slogged through a rice paddy. His long stringy hair grew from a dirty red bandanna tied over his head Geronimo-style.

I had waited a long time to see him. Twenty-seven years of fitful sleep while nightmares and pain from little pieces of shrapnel floating near my spine reminded me to keep looking. And looking at him now, he seemed no more real that the picture I carried in my head of Cronkle lying in my arms, his hot guts oozing blood over his lap and mine.

The last thing I whispered to Cronkle before he died was, "I'll get the son of a bitch for you!" And finally, here he was, stoned out

21

of his mind in a cheap strip joint outside Topeka, Kansas. I'd found him.

The bartender saw me looking at him and, as he wiped his hands on a dirty apron, said, "Hey mister, if you want to talk to him, you'll have to get here sooner. He's out of it now. Gets like this every day. He just sits there not talking. Some woman comes and picks him up about six every night. Some woman! He's here every day and she doesn't ever forget."

Finding him here like this didn't surprise me. I'd looked just like him a few short months before. I'd given up on everything. I drank 'til drinking didn't do any good. Tried drugs too but I never could find any that did just what I wanted them to do. I either got too high or too stoned or too depressed. Booze did it most of the time. It made me numb enough to quit thinking and feeling but then I ended up in a VA Hospital. My kidneys quit working and I turned yellow. They told me to lay off the booze or I'd die. Dying sounded good. And I'd be right back out there now, trying to do myself with a jag, except getting sober caused me to remember my oath to Cronkle. So I figured that before I died, I should even up the score for my dead friend.

My mistake was not pulling out the pistol I carry and wasting him right there on the spot. Without thinking. That's how we did it in 'Nam. You didn't think and you didn't feel. It didn't matter once you learned how. It would have been easy to do him right then but maybe I'd lost my edge and didn't know it. I'd thought a thousand times since 'Nam that I'd like to do somebody. Maybe the real desire wasn't there anymore. Maybe I lost the ability to do it without thinking.

See, right at the moment my hand touched the gun in my pocket, I remembered why we called him Eyes. I would have forgotten his real name was Matt except I found a letter I wrote home to my sister. That was before Cronkle died. I told my sister in the letter how Eyes got his name.

We were humpin', that's marching, through this vill' one day. Matt is in the lead walking point. There's Vietnamese all around us. Mamasans, Papasans, kids and a whole lot of guys the wrong age. You know, the age to be either in the ARVN outfits or the NVA or Viet Cong outfits. We were all feeling kinda spooked. Then Matt steps back from point and says to me real low, "They got guns."

I glanced around and didn't see any guns but I had the hair-raising feeling he was right.

23

We were near the middle of this little vill' and I yelled, "hit the tree line!"

Guys started running and Vietnamese started shooting. Only one of our guys got hit in the back of the leg. We called in 'boo-coo' shit and that vill' was no longer part of any map. And if it hadn't been for Matt, we'd have all been dead. Me and the first team leader wrote him up for a medal. Later the Captain called a formation and called Matt up front.

"Lance Corporal Barrow, there are no medals for seeing well, although I think in your case there should be. I want to thank and congratulate you. Your eyes saved your squad."

What stuck was, "Eyes saved the squad." We clapped and cheered and pounded him in the back. That's when he announced he would be the squads' permanent point man. Because of his superior vision he'd walk up front to spot booby-traps and ambushes.

And he did. Eyes always took point. The old guys forgot how and the new guys never learned. Eyes liked his hero status. He was always being the good guy. One time out in the field this new guy—I don't remember his name, he got killed a week after this thing I'm telling about took place—pulled off his boots and his pink, stateside feet were a mass of blisters. Somebody asked him if he'd been changing his socks.

He said, "Hell, I ain't wearing any socks. I thought they'd cause blisters."

Everybody laughed at this dumb ass but then Eyes pulled out this brand new pair of socks and gave them to the new guy. He did stuff like that and here I am wondering how I'm going to kill him and I'm remembering the good shit. I should have offed him before I started thinking.

Then I remembered the time Cronkle and I went on R & R to Manila. That was only about two weeks before he got it. We had a good time. We both got girls from some GI joint called Sam's or George's or something. And we spent most of the time in bed. It just felt good to lie down under a roof on a mattress and not worry about your ass getting blown away while you slept. But we stayed pretty uptight. You couldn't leave all that shit behind just because your ass was wrapped in a clean white sheet.

The second night we were there we got drunk and went home to the hotel to sack out. I just got my eyes closed when the Filipino girl that Cronkle was with, I think her name was Luz, came running into my room.

"Come back quick GI," she yelled. "Your friend, he go crazy maybe."

I went running down to his room and there stood Cronkle standing naked with his K-bar in his hand. Feathers were still floating in the air and scattered all over the room. He looked like he felt pretty silly and said, "Guess I had a little dream."

That was all he ever said about it and I didn't mind and he stayed drunk 'til we got back to the bush.

When we got back, Eyes does this totally chicken shit thing and Cronkle ends up dead. And not just an easy dead. His death wasn't fast and neat, you know, like you'd always like it to be.

We were humpin' a trail and there was a big explosion. It knocked me down and I remember seeing Cronkle fly over my head. Fly, just like he'd sprouted wings. It seemed funny then as I lay on my back trying to get my breath back. Here's old Cronkle in the middle of a firefight taking time out for soaring. I snapped back to reality when the screaming started. God, I hate screaming. It's unmanly and weird. Stays in your ears too long afterwards.

I checked first to see if I had any leaks and couldn't find any. That's because I got hit in the back. Then I looked behind me to see where Cronkle landed. I saw he was hurt bad. He was lying on the back moving his arms and legs slow like he was a bug in water.

I crawled over to him. His pants and shirt had been blown off and I saw gray gut hanging from his belly. I almost couldn't make myself say anything to him. Then I said something real stupid.

"Hang on Cronkle. Looks like you got a little hole. We'll get Doc to patch you up. Corpsman up! Corpsman up here god-dammit!" I yelled.

I knew when I saw him that he was as good as dead. No way he'd last 'til a dustoff arrived.

"Help me buddy! I'm scared," Cronkle whispered and bloody foam oozed out of his mouth.

That's when I lifted him in my arms and tried to scoop up his gut and put it back in, but it wouldn't fit. I just sat there rocking him and holding my hand over that bloody mess, telling him that I would even up the score with Eyes. I didn't know that Eyes got medevac'd too.

They sent me to a hospital ship and tried to get all the shrapnel but left some in me. I was sent back to duty and never saw Eyes again, until this joint in Topeka. I just stood there looking down at him trying to remember how much I hated him for Cronkle's sake. I tried to remember that I was going to kill him, but I kept remembering the other shit instead.

There was a night on Hill 881 up by the DMZ. I read somewhere recently that we took that hill and gave it back four times. Well, this was the first time we took it. We lost over a hundred guys getting to the top through some rough fighting. . .hand to hand and all.

After the hill was secured, Cronkle, Eyes and I ended up on a listening post together. We all figured we'd die there because the NVA were all over. We were whispering in the dark to keep our brave up. We talked about women, round-eyed women, the kind back home.

"Man, this chick I got at home is so sweet she'd make you shitbirds cry." Eyes said.

Cronkle razzed him. "Hell man, you ain't ever been with a sweet girl. She's probably some old bar room hooker."

Eyes rummaged around in a beat up billfold and pulled out a snapshot and handed it to Cronkle. He bent way down in our foxhole and flicked his lighter to see it.

I bent over too. "You must have stolen the picture, Eyes. She's sharp!"

"Turn the picture over," he said.

Cronkle flipped it over and read the back.

"Matt, I'll miss you a lot. Don't forget all our good times and don't forget the night at you know where. Love, forever, Connie."

"Hey, no shit!" Cronkle said. "Where'd you spend the night?"

"Oh, at some motel outside of town. The Topeka Inn, I think."

"Decent, man!" I said.

"Yeah! Decent." Cronkle added.

That picture was why I remembered he was from here, and now I wasn't too sure how to pull off what I'd come to do.

I looked at my watch. It was going on five o'clock. If somebody came after him at six, I didn't want to be around. I damn sure didn't want it to be Connie in the picture. I carry a five-inch fold up knife. It would have been easy to stick it under his ribs and up into his heart. He probably wouldn't have made any noise. Shock sets in immediately. Noise wouldn't have mattered anyhow. I'd planned on doing myself when I was done so I wasn't afraid of getting caught. Instead, I put my arm on his shoulder and shook him.

"Hey, Eyes! It's me, look at me!" I guess I kinda hissed the words.

He didn't move. He just sat there like he was dead. That pissed me off a little.

"Hey, you asshole. It's me. Talk to me!"

He turned so fast, I jumped. Then he stared right into my eyes the same way he'd been staring at the palm tree and he kept staring without saying anything for a long time. Finally, his mouth opened.

"Where's Cronkle?" He asked in a flat, slurred voice.

I stared at him, my hand on the gun in my pocket and then I said, "Cronkle's dead. You got him killed."

His mouth sagged. His eyes went even dimmer. "Dead? Is he really dead? Are you sure?"

"Yeah, I'm sure." I said.

"He shouldn't of been on point. You knew he couldn't see very well."

"Sure he shouldn't have. He was there because you wouldn't be, remember?" I said.

"No, man. He was on point because you got pissed off at him. Remember he fell asleep during our last night of ambush. You were so mad you hit him in the mouth. Then, instead of writing him up, you told him he could walk point the next day. I told you not to let him."

Eyes couldn't have hit me harder with a sledge hammer. I knew then that he was right. I remembered putting Cronkle on point. I must have changed it all around in my head while I was on the hospital ship. Somehow I

30

had decided Cronkle had died because Eyes wouldn't take point that day. There I stood, right in the middle of twenty-seven years of shit I had caused myself.

That's when I ordered a drink. And another, and another. I went home with Eyes that night and stayed. He's got a woman. I don't remember her name. Me and Eyes don't talk much about stuff. We mostly just sit and drink. It's what hurts the least.

HIDING

Hiding in the night like a mouse
   waiting for the cat to pass,
like my dog hid
   before the shot was fired,
like love hid
   from my first marriage,
like peace hides
   when Corporal Ives' maggoty head
invades my dreams.

Like courage hides
   when life invites.

TO: G. WASHUTT, USMC
KIA 1967

I see you standing in a Nam-time mist,
    huddled like a jungle quarterback
calling end runs, life you win, death you lose.
    Your eyes peer out like hidden VC
from behind your camouflaged face,
    you a real leader to those who follow
through a Hell of booby-traps and
    bloody ambushes.
We share peaches from one can,
    plastic spoon clicking against your teeth
as Goose Creek and Wyoming mountains
    slide easily from your tongue and for
a little moment you frame gentle farm boy eyes
    in Marine issue glasses and we are creek kin,
mine a scant two hundred miles from yours,
back in the world where we both once lived.

Ten years later, my wife sips stale coffee
    in a Sheridan café while I drive
to the hillside trailer, gray like a pagoda
    with brown dog turds standing guard.
Your Old Man covers fear with gruffness,
    I hide mine behind a ten-year wall.

$\rightarrow$

Mother Washutt, graying, sends me with tired
    eyes to the holy shrine.
A hometown boy I never knew peers out from
    between Zenith rabbit ears while a pimpled
face beneath promises forty percent chance of rain
    that night.
A Marine that wasn't you wears Dress Blues.
    "Son, this pitcher'll make your mama proud
someday!"
    A polished Silver Star hangs like a God's Eye
over your daddy's ancient Sears recliner.
    In this foreign place old reels start playing
my movies on the wall by the big hall mirror.
    My jungle tongue won't speak of Goose Creek
ghosts and I stare at the floor while Mama wrings
her hands.

I walk out cold like I walked in and drive
    ten more years to a paint-chipped table where
my wife sips more coffee while I visit my past.
    At the wall I find your silent name
and reach out to touch you one last time.

WASHUTT:
MY VOICE IS NOT STILLED

Listen!
    Once I cursed at jungle vines
    as I crawled in Vietnam.
I was the warrior Prince and sang
my song near the DMZ
    I met the enemy at Cam Lo
    and screamed at him in fighting rage.
He died silently on an ugly hill
and I died silently beside him.
    In the terrible thunder of war
    We waited unspeaking of time.

Listen!
    Now I laugh with mountain trout
    in mirrored pools of Goose Creek.
I sing with summer winds
strumming tops of Bighorn pines.
    I whisper springtime meadow secrets
    to dancing bees in crocus ballrooms.
I cry tears that fall with leaves of quakin' asp'.
    In the wintertime I speak
    the soft swoosh of a child's sled
on fresh Wyoming snow.
I wait unspeaking of time.

A BAD NIGHT

Hiding on a 25-watt island,
specters gathering,
garbling unveiled threats,
jabbing crooked digits
into fear staled breath

Posses' form, mounted black,
galloping across bridges
spanning turbulent shreds
of unused sleep.

Hold, hold, bit by tiny bit,
clinging tight to iced slices
of an unpromised tomorrow
residing farther down
some rutted road that stretches
from here to there.

PROMISES

I wear my strangeness
like a badge,
    and watch others notice it.
The catch is that when I crawl into bed at night,
    it turns and bites me.
    I check the windows
to see who's looking in
    and convince my wife that it was an accident
    when I fell asleep with the light on.
I try to resign from the bizarre
    and ghosts stare into my eyes at night,
    daring me to leave them,
screaming that if I do,
    they will deposit maggoty smells
    into my nostrils as I sleep
I promise myself that I'm sane,
    I'm in control,
    I am the dreamer
and try to find trust in my own promises.

Robert Sasse

GREY GHOST'S SON

Prayless hands fidget
through unforgiving days
while chemo drops
like Viet Cong across the wire.
A small confused voice, "Why?"
as white coats slide around on icy hopes
and the gray warrior falls
into a molasses world.

COYOTES FADE

I sit on a hill of lava stones
peering through thorny mesquite bushes.
Raven wings pound decibels,
stirring dusty pasts.

Was that me born gently
to Montana meadows,
yet me raging at the screams
of mortars and men

and still me
marveling and crying
while my son emerged
from innocent womb
to my cold world?
Is there a footprint

somewhere other than
this breezy ridge
that marks a trek
across my soul?
In a faraway past

coyotes sit
beside my father's grave,
howling at a rising moon.

$\rightarrow$

I hear his voice
and climb
down from the hill
searching for days
not yet made.
I see them,

though not quite
before they start to fade.

WE WERE PRIDEFUL WARRIORS

We beat the plowshares of our childhood into
swords and marched like blind men to
    the field of battle.
    We were baptized there by whining shards
of metal, and ugly mounds
    of torn flesh
    and torn souls. We watched babies die alone
and mothers die and futures die
    leaving only
    the pain of hope for those who stood. We
walked from those mangled fields
    of torn rice
    and tattered bamboo past the caskets of our
friends. At home the air was
    free of screams
    and we could breathe but when those gentle
    winds of peace blew against
    our wounded parts
    we hid, afraid to meet the demons in our
heads. We cowered in corners
    of our minds
    and slapped at images that had swallowed
up our youth. We cried real tears
    that would not
    drown our dreams. Bitterness and despair
grew and became the garden of our pain.

$\rightarrow$

41

We couldn't reach out because we knew
 that what we'd seen and
    what we'd done had
colored us with
    garish shame and left exposed our guilt. In
a cautionary tale we were prideful
    warriors, our lance
    against the enemy's bowel. We fought with
the weapons we'd been given; anger,
    ruthlessness and hate
    and the weapons turned and pierced us
through. On that piece of bloodied
    land we walked
    like shadows, unable to affect our
cheapened lives. Why speak of war as
    bastard? Perhaps some
    vision of righteousness was served by that
devil's fodder. But know this! From
    outside a war,
    a sense of life lived full hearkens to a baser
urge and hides the preciousness
    of breath and
    those who take the beckon will find the
basement of their souls where they will one
    day cry alone.

RETURN FROM HELL

*(I was reminded of the post-traumatic stress faced by
returning warriors today.)*

I see you standing in the mist of an autumn funk,
your shoulders fallen,
laying in the taint of bad yesterdays,
the pain of life out pacing the worth
of another tomorrow.
What gruesome rooms hide behind your eyes,
luring you into places your mind and heart and soul
can't follow?

Youth for you has soured, wine made undrinkable
even as your thirst for peace has been supplanted by
more vile tastes of anger and rage and hopelessness.
What has called you to this quagmire of poison life,
what distant drum guided your pounding feet?

We look on,
those who stand away from the slash of bloody war,
not knowing or understanding or even caring of the
weight you will bear far past your time
of standing on lines of death and mayhem
and murderous fear.
We cannot, will not,
feel the emptiness of human hope
that you carry to your sleeping place.

COLD MOUNTAIN WATER

Sometimes I sit
near a river in my mind,
willows and cottonwoods
standing placidly on its banks,
cold mountain water
sliding over hidden stones
speaking of sacred things.
I am an observer
or maybe an intruder;
the stillness doesn't invite a busy head.
I stay and let the gentleness of a morning breeze
make me a part of what I see.

The water chatters
as it washes over the scars on my soul
and soothes the wounded places
of my heart. Images of lost friends
and scorned enemies float past.
I bid them well,
knowing they are no longer
rulers of my life.

This is a hallowed place,
full of hope where the ripples
show me images of gifts
flowing into my days
and I am at peace
with the lessons of my life.

GLENDA IN NEW MEXICO

Dark clouds wait on timbered ridges to
    slide beneath the sun.
A north wind hunts the canyon, preying
    on tumble weeds
and whipping juniper branches into ritual
    dances of winter.
Our campfire makes its own small clouds
    of smoke that scatter
like javalinas running down the arroyo. She
    huddles tight against my arm
and asks if yucca ever blooms in April.

GLENDA IN THE RAIN

Like vibrant drums
    looking for dancers
        raindrops beat a tattoo
            against the metal roof.
Leaves do splashy dances
    And little rivers conspire
        to join and create wet
            havoc in the drive.
The world tightens and
    loneliness skulks nearby
        watching over my shoulder
            through the graying pane.
She stands by
    my side saving
        the day from
            a hidden despair.

GLENDA IN MONTANA

Kind mountain breezes
slide
over mossy granite
fall
on tall, sweet grasses,
wind
'round deft strokes
of Indian Paint Brush

Quiet, green stones
bend
upward, slide kisses
across
silver trees laying
against
a cloud dappled surface
and the water sings.

Burning light filters through
fluttering
cottonwood fingers on a
hillside.
Rain split by leaves
hesitates
to drop on goose bumped arms.

$\rightarrow$

Mountain sunlight
pours
over gray and balding
heads of sage.
Cold shafts of moon
vibrate
with snowy howls of coyote

She is warm against
my chest. Her scent
is earth
and life.

MARRIAGE

The efforts of two,
exponentially
gathering heights, she but half,
he the other and yet more than the sum
of various aspirations.

He, to the moon, to the moon,
she with her feet on the ground
they, to walk and to fly,
fingers aligned,
strength of the two backed beast

to airy places
and to some made of stone,
to hold tightly with nary a cling
'til dust do them part

or not.

MAZIE

Her fuzzy bulk nudges me as we sit
beneath a juniper tree. I tear a corner
from my tuna sandwich and she quits
considering the sound of bunny feet to take
it gently from my hand. Her gruffness
almost hides a slurpy kiss. I think about a
forlorn deserted pup saved from a short
cruel life and she thinks about dog things,
unconcerned. I stroke her soft black hair
not yet knowing our time together is almost
done.

BUFFALO IN
YELLOWSTONE PARK

Shaggy son of prairie
fields
trudging through this
snowbound
corner of America's
guilty
conscience, steamy
bursts
blowing through nostrils
that do
not measure air by
freedom
but by endless steps
on trails
cleaved through
passing time.
Ten thousand prayers
have borne
your fate as you
walked through the
European rape.
You swaddled
in robes an
Earthy Nation, from
birth
to barren scaffold, stark
against dynamic
skies.

$\rightarrow$

Robert Sasse

Tatanka, as
you walk on by
here's a begging prayer.
Take me with you so
the people might live.

MARY'S WINGS

The call was actually a mistake. My mother's lips tightened as she listened to the phone. "Mrs. Pincher, my brother Van fell off the hog barn roof and I think he's hurt real bad!"

Sandy Horvack mistakenly thought my mother had been a nurse but it wouldn't have made a difference. She wanted nothing to do with blood and pain so she told my father to go check on Van. That's when he looked at me and said, "Guess you could come along, he's your friend."

I was twelve years old and the lingering question has always been the same. Would my father have asked me along if he'd known we would find Van dead, lying in his father's arms with flecks of vomit running from slack lips, down over his chin to pool like lumpy, yellow pancake batter on the faded linoleum floor of the Horvack's kitchen?

In my ranch boy's world, chickens died, cows died, good horses died and of course, favorite dogs died. Seeing a friend, who had been completely animated just the day before, now lying slack jawed and lifeless in the same yellow and black flannel shirt I had grabbed in a game of tag the day before, was a new and awesome experience. I was horribly and totally fascinated.

I had expected more drama--maybe a death angel or at least a harp-playing angel to hover in recognition of my friend's departure from his body.

The scene was so bizarre, I didn't feel anything, not for me or Van's father or his sister or my own father, for that matter. He stood beside Mr. Horvack with a hand laid gently on his shoulder saying, "Damn, Brian. Oh damn."

He should have said something about the death while we drove home. If he did, my mind didn't register it. Instead we stopped at the barn and threw loose alfalfa hay to the cows and horses without a word between us. The sweet smell of the alfalfa did not overwhelm the sourness of Van's vomit that still clung to my olfactory mechanisms.

I was fiddling with that memory while I was sitting on a cheap, plastic chair in a room painted an unnatural shade of green at the Fort Harrison Veterans Hospital in Helena waiting for a psychologist to appear. Old men with rubber helmets doing the Thorazine shuffle wandered aimlessly past the door. Every breath of air was ripe with smells of stale urine and antiseptics. Seeing the sick and infirm in the hospital left me weak and unsure of my capacity to function.

I was about to sneak away when he called me into a room where he sat in an overstuffed recliner. His hands were folded into a prayer steeple and he nodded toward a hard wooden chair. I took the bait and sat.

As he crushed out the butt of a Parliament cigarette in an ashtray that he promptly hid in a drawer, he said, "Perhaps we can help you solve some of your problems, find your way back into society. You'll be more comfortable."

I was polite enough not to point out that his premise was all fucked up. Comfortable I didn't need, and the only real problem in my life was that the Park County Sheriff's deputies picked me up when I went to Livingston for groceries. I didn't want back into society. I didn't belong there. Vietnam had seen to that. Society was full of people who could never know what I had seen and done in the name of serving my country.

My children thought they were saving me by convincing a judge that I was a danger to myself. Perhaps I'd walked into my own ambush? Well, maybe, but now I just wanted back into the Crazy Mountains where I felt safe and the world was slow enough to make sense.

The shrink stared at me from behind a pair of thick horn-rimmed glasses, like some brain-damaged owl. "Do you think we should start by examining some of your Vietnam experiences?"

Do I think I want my foot run over by a Mack truck? Do I live this way because I'm an aging flower child with a psychosis? Hadn't anybody told this quack that it's a full time job keeping the ghosts in a box and I would be crazy to turn them loose in front of strangers who asked stupid questions?

Maybe I would have answered him, that is, before the thing with Mary. With her, my life was almost normal and the spooks were at bay. A wife, two kids, a house with mostly paid rent and a whole string of jobs. Not Ward and June Cleaver's life but not bad. Mary and I were hiking on top of the dividing ridge between Trespass Creek and Campfire Lake. It's one of those sacred little corners of the earth where you are as likely to see an eagle from above as below. Our eyes could see what they saw as their giant wings, filled with mountain air, carried them sliding across ridges in search of marmots hiding in the rocks below.

Mary wanted to see the old goat trap where the Fish and Game captured mountain goat babies and tagged them. It was a steep, tough climb down to a pen made of sheep wire and scraggy pieces of wood gathered from a nearby stand of winter stunted pine. The trap clung to the ridge top precipitously above a two hundred foot cliff.

On the way I told her about a mule that had gone over the edge with a load of fish destined for Hindu Lake. She laughed and said maybe they were flying fish. She was adopting some of my macabre sense of humor.

Afterwards, when she was gone, I was sleeping one night beside Rock Creek Lake and woke up with a bear's muzzle right next to my face. I smelled his fetid breath as he was sniffing to see if I was alive. At first I thought it was my dog, Tuffy. He used to do that when I was small. He'd just stand and stare at my face until I woke up. When my mind registered that a bear was staring into my eyes, I thought of the first time Mary and I made love. Weird, huh?

It was six months after I got back from Vietnam when I met Mary. I hadn't given up on the ranch yet, but it was going downhill. My father was already dead and my desire to accomplish anything was almost dead.

Like a fantasy wrapped in freshness and laughter, she came to the ranch one winter day and went with me to feed cattle. The harness on the horses jingled and their breath left small clouds in the cold air as we slid across crisp snow with a sled. The runners swooshed and squeaked and Mary's cheeks were red and her smile was perfect and just then, my life was okay. For the first time the ugly jungle wasn't following me around. We made love that night and she became the reality that squeezed Vietnam from my soul.

And then later, when my soul was an empty pit, some big, foul-breathed bear made me remember those delicious moments. By then I had become as much a part of the mountains as the bear was and he must have made me out as bitter meat because he left me there to shake Mary from my head.

Once it was easy to clear my head. Up the Sedan, out of Wilsal, there was an old watering trough under a big willow tree. While we were in high school, Duane and Art and I would go out there at night and listen to KOMA out of

Oklahoma City and drink skunky tasting Highlander beer and laugh about our troubles. After we graduated, Duane stepped on a booby trap and Art died in an ambush, their bodies so perforated that neither mother saw an open casket.

I went back to see the old watering trough not long ago. Walked twenty miles one night to get there and it was gone. In its place was a big plastic tank, filled by an electric pump and everything was different. Duane and Art would have hated the change as much as I did and we couldn't have laughed there anymore.

I followed that bear like he was a nightmare clinging to my psyche. It was a moonlit night and he moved slowly, climbing across a big scree pile, making flat pieces of shale sound like breaking plates. A couple of times he stopped and stood up, warning me not to follow him, hoping I would forget about him, stirring memories that were better left alone. It's not like I was going to kick his ass. I just wanted to see where he went after screwing up someone's night.

My father brought a bear home once on the back of Dell, his favorite horse. Not many horses will pack a bear but old Dell did. It was a dark, overcast fall day. Maybe I was nine or ten years old. I was playing out by the haystacks with trucks and tractors I'd made by nailing bits of wood together and he came up the road from the creek, the bear slung across the saddle while he walked in front of him. I was so excited I was trembling.

I knew my father would tell me a wonderful story about killing that bear; how just in the nick of time he was able to get a shot off and save himself, but instead all he said was "Hi, son." Maybe there wasn't a story.

It was like that when Packard got killed. He took his squad out, called in an air strike and they dropped napalm on his head. Where's the story in that? Mary was a story. She was like the beautiful Princess who married the wrong Prince and she didn't live happily ever after. She was a story when our children were born. I watched them emerge from her body like angels from the clouds and we cried together from sheer joy and both times I was afraid my tears wouldn't stop. Mary used to say I had dams of sadness behind my eyes that would burst one day and maybe drown us both.

We both cried again when we knew the ranch was gone, swallowed by unpaid debt and unpaid karma. Afterward, she touched me and said, "its okay."

It seemed like everything I did made things worse. I took a squad out once. Nine guys followed me into an ambush like chicks behind a hen. They were good Marines, tired of Vietnam but always ready to do what they were asked. The wet, soupy blackness of a jungle night turned inside out and when the med-evac chopper had finally come and gone, it was dawn and I was standing alone, waiting for the sun to turn another day into a steamy oven that would bake me in a stew of guilt and remorse. I sure made things worse for those guys.

"We'll be all right," Mary said in her soft, forgiving voice. We moved to White Sulfur Springs and I worked at the saw mill. Mary worked in a store and sometimes there was enough money and sometimes there wasn't.

When Murphy got killed I had enough money to do R and R and I needed to get away from the jungle for a bit. Too much of that stuff and you start getting gungey, you know, a little weird. I was supposed to do Singapore and then Lieutenant Edwards had a chance to go to Hawaii to see his wife. He was short of money so I lent him four hundred bucks and stayed in Vietnam. I know the Lieutenant was good for the loan.

He got back and stood up at the wrong time. Crazy bastard! When you're pinned down in a rice paddy and the shit is coming down, you don't ever stand up and say, "Hit the tree line!" Maybe things didn't go so good with his wife.

I grabbed his legs and was holding them when he took four rounds in the chest. It felt like when I tackled Art once during football practice. Art started hopping up and down and almost got away. Maybe Lieutenant Edwards almost got away too but he collapsed in a heap on top of me and I was staring into his eyes when his lights went out.

I started losing it at the saw mill. Seemed like everybody set out just to piss me off. One day, the saws started sounding like screams. I smacked the foreman in the mouth and walked all the way to the top of the Big Belt Mountains.

Mary wasn't mad when I got home and we moved to Billings. On a really bad day when I wasn't feeling good about myself I stood on top of the rim rocks near the airport and tried to make myself jump into oblivion at the bottom and I swear to God, at the very moment I saw myself airborne, I saw Mary. Not an apparition, but there in the flesh on a street below the cliffs, getting out of her car and walking into a house she was getting paid to clean. I fell in a heap and bawled like a baby.

That Lieutenant used to play poker with us. He was a regular guy, except he didn't know how to bluff. Once he tried to steal a hundred dollar pot with a pair of sixes. I held three kings and I called him. He actually blushed when he showed that little pair. It was a look like getting caught at something stupid. That's how he looked when he collapsed on top of me and his face was right next to mine. He knew he shouldn't have stood up. Those must be some sad last thoughts.

"Oops, I shouldn't have been on the hog barn roof. Uh, oh, I shouldn't have listened to that damn major. Damn! Wish I hadn't called in this air strike. Oh shit, maybe I shouldn't have stood up."

I know the question. What did my Mary think as she was falling from that ridge top at the goat trap into the thin mountain air toward the stones below? "Oops, never travel with a man who's lost a squad." It took me almost an hour to climb down to her. She lay between two boulders, crumpled and broken like a used up doll. I climbed down off that mountain with her in my arms, mad because she'd left without saying good-bye. She wasn't heavy.

Murphy was heavy. While I carried him I kept thinking about dropping him on top of the major, like when the lieutenant fell on me. I did, and that major tried to get me court-martialed.

Poor old Sheriff Bates looked like he was afraid as he stared at Mary's body. She wasn't bloody like Murphy, just bent in places where she shouldn't have been.

Maybe carrying her into the sheriff's office and laying her on that ugly, green counter wasn't such a good idea. I wish now I'd left her on the mountain where she would have been at home. At her funeral my kids cried a lot. I wanted to sit with them but I couldn't do it. My sister was there, comforting them and I left knowing she would finish raising them.

I left when they had the stupid memorial service at Camp Carroll too. Bayoneted rifles were standing in the ground with helmets on them to represent guys who'd bought a bullet or stepped into the oblivion of a booby trap. The rifles were M-14s, not the new plastic pieces of shit that jammed every other round. I was too preoccupied with stealing one of those good weapons sticking in the dirt to think about the dead buddies they had replaced.

Later after Mary's funeral was over I went to the cemetery. It sits on a hill overlooking the river. The sagebrush is kept outside the perimeter but the grass inside is dry and yellow most of the year. Mary was there, buried amongst people she had known because of me. She ended up in a garden full of strangers. At least Murphy got shipped home to his mother.

Mary had been my balm, salve for my scarred-up soul. She had made me whole and capable of life. And the best this shrink in front of me could ask was, "Do you ever have any feelings about hurting yourself or anyone else?"

I stared at him, at that porcine face with watery eyes and a mouth that had never twisted into a scream of despair. I didn't like him and I didn't think he knew the right questions.

"You know," I said to him, "I believe that Van dove off that hog barn roof and I think Mary almost flew."

BURNING HAIR
AT BRANDING TIME

I was born near mountains
that hung like jewels on a blue bodice
and clear lakes that soaked up
granite cliffs in noonday sun.
My swaddling was tall grass on an open hill
where sunflowers peered down
like alpine nannies
while meadowlarks sang lullabies.

My backyard was two miles high
and wide as a child's mind.
I ate fat raspberries that grew by cool spring
water and played with wiggly worms.
Their slime dried like snot on my chubby
hands and I watched butterflies
and stared at chickens in the barn.
There was no time then,
only fresh churned butter
and home cured bacon to mark a day.

I trudged off to a one room school, its walls
saturated with the dust of a thousand chalks,
and a pump clanging to lift noontime drinks
from a hand dug well
while a teacher with a sharp edged ruler
served frontier justice.

A first kiss behind the woodshed was sweet
like wild honey and filled with promises
I knew nothing of.
I learned arithmetic and
how to dance the Virginia Reel
and how to crawl up a mountain crag
where barren stones were stacked in the lap of
benevolent clouds.

I walked through tunnels of tall pines and
knew songs about freedom of my soul.
There were summer days when alfalfa fields
smelled like a Sunday treat
and fat Rainbow trout hid behind granite
stones and willow shoots.
There were dogs, furry friends who never
betrayed a secret or a sin
and taught me how to cry at death and rail
against the fates.
Aunts and uncles and cousins and
grandparents
clung like morning dew to my family tree.

Stacks of fried chicken and dripping
marshmallows celebrated July Fourth days
and those days seemed young
as my father, gruff but gentle,
nudged me toward the path of men.
I learned to seed the fallow land
and breathe the smell of burning hair at
branding time.

Robert Sasse

→

My skin was dark from summer sun and in the
fall, aspen leaves jumped from trees to kiss the
gentle soil, then lay like colored patches in my
mother's sewing basket, reds and yellows and
brown like leather boots.

I learned to hunt amongst those fallen pages of
summer's story, took deer for winter's meat
and left blood on that hallowed ground.
I waited for the first snow to paint the world
new and white and clean,
when harnesses came out and jingled
and sled runners cracked across the open
snow, pulled by the steaming
nostrils of our horses.
The wind blew and cold came and the milk
cows stood in the freezing barn
while we made rhythms with squirting milk.

Soon I waited for ground hogs and learned to
trust buttercups and crocuses.
My feet belonged to giants as I tromped
through springtime mud and watched my
mountains shed their hoary coats and shine
with the power of rebirth and I was reborn
each day beneath a blue Montana sky
where prairies promised freedom
and mountains spoke of hope.

I was young there once.

SWEAT LODGE

Canvas womb of willow
ribs, gentle mother, to earth
returns my sweat. Ancient
stones in baptisms of hot
and holy breath. Prayers
soar like pairs
of spotted eagles.
Small cloud of cool
tart smoke, my heart
is good, beats like buffalo
drums, sounds
of sacred songs,
my heart is good.

ABOUT THE AUTHOR

Robert Sasse served in Vietnam with the Third Battalion, Ninth Regiment, Third Marine Division in 1966-1967. He earned a Bronze Star with Combat V, and served in a unit that earned a Presidential Unit Citation.

He now lives in southwestern New Mexico with his wife, and writes about his experiences both in Vietnam and healing from the aftermath of combat.

Robert was raised on a ranch at the foot of the Crazy Mountains in Montana and has been a rodeo clown and bullfighter, an auctioneer, a policeman and tried his hand at many other things. After returning from Vietnam, his ability to function deteriorated until at age forty he found sobriety and help with post-traumatic stress disorder. Eventually he discovered the power of healing through the expression of poetry and prose. This selection of stories and poetry reflect his healing as he goes from raw images of war, to a serenity that only comes with finding inner peace. He hopes to share these images with other veterans and those who suffer from their own private "Vietnam" and the resulting depression and despair.